Marriage

D0726792

Church House Publishing

Published by   Church House Publishing
                  Church House
                  Great Smith Street
                  London SW1P 3NZ

Copyright ©   *The Archbishops' Council 2000*

                  First published 2000

                  Sixth impression 2004

                  0 7151 2038 7

Printed and bound by ArklePrint Ltd, Northampton
on 80 gsm Dutchman Ivory

Typeset in Gill Sans
by John Morgan and Shirley Thompson/Omnific
Designed by Derek Birdsall RDI

The material in this booklet is extracted from *Common Worship:
Pastoral Services*. It comprises:

¶   the Marriage Service;
¶   extracts from the Marriage Service within a Celebration of
    Holy Communion;
¶   Notes to the Marriage Service;
¶   extracts from Supplementary Texts to Marriage;
¶   General Rules.

For other material, page references to *Common Worship:
Pastoral Services* are supplied.

Pagination   This booklet has two sets of page numbers. The outer numbers
                are the booklet's own page numbers, while the inner numbers
                near the centre of most pages refer to the equivalent pages in
                Common Worship: Pastoral Services.

Contents

*In preparing for the service, the minister should refer to the
full provisions of the Marriage section in* Common Worship:
Pastoral Services *(pages 101–172).*

The Marriage Service

¶ *Pastoral Introduction*

This may be read by those present before the service begins.

A wedding is one of life's great moments, a time of solemn commitment as well as good wishes, feasting and joy. St John tells us how Jesus shared in such an occasion at Cana, and gave there a sign of new beginnings as he turned water into wine.

Marriage is intended by God to be a creative relationship, as his blessing enables husband and wife to love and support each other in good times and in bad, and to share in the care and upbringing of children. For Christians, marriage is also an invitation to share life together in the spirit of Jesus Christ. It is based upon a solemn, public and life-long covenant between a man and a woman, declared and celebrated in the presence of God and before witnesses.

On this their wedding day the bride and bridegroom face each other, make their promises and receive God's blessing. You are witnesses of the marriage, and express your support by your presence and your prayers. Your support does not end today: the couple will value continued encouragement in the days and years ahead of them.

Love is patient; love is kind; love is not envious or boastful or arrogant or rude. It does not insist on its own way; it is not irritable or resentful; it does not rejoice in wrongdoing, but rejoices in the truth. It bears all things, believes all things, hopes all things, endures all things.

1 Corinthians 13.4-7

The Marriage Service

Structure

For Notes, see pages 38–40.

The Marriage Service

¶ *Introduction*

The Welcome

*The minister welcomes the people using these
or other appropriate words*

The grace of our Lord Jesus Christ,
the love of God,
and the fellowship of the Holy Spirit
be with you

All **and also with you.**

This sentence may be used

God is love, and those who live in love live in God
and God lives in them. *1 John 4.16*

This prayer may be said

All **God of wonder and of joy:
grace comes from you,
and you alone are the source of life and love.
Without you, we cannot please you;
without your love, our deeds are worth nothing.
Send your Holy Spirit,
and pour into our hearts
       that most excellent gift of love,
that we may worship you now
with thankful hearts
and serve you always with willing minds;
through Jesus Christ our Lord.
Amen.**

A hymn may be sung.

Preface

These words or those on page 15 are used

In the presence of God, Father, Son and Holy Spirit,
we have come together
to witness the marriage of N and N,
to pray for God's blessing on them,
to share their joy
and to celebrate their love.

Marriage is a gift of God in creation
through which husband and wife may know the grace of God.
It is given
that as man and woman grow together in love and trust,
they shall be united with one another in heart, body and mind,
as Christ is united with his bride, the Church.

The gift of marriage brings husband and wife together
in the delight and tenderness of sexual union
and joyful commitment to the end of their lives.
It is given as the foundation of family life
in which children are [born and] nurtured
and in which each member of the family,
in good times and in bad,
may find strength, companionship and comfort,
and grow to maturity in love.

Marriage is a way of life made holy by God,
and blessed by the presence of our Lord Jesus Christ
with those celebrating a wedding at Cana in Galilee.
Marriage is a sign of unity and loyalty
which all should uphold and honour.
It enriches society and strengthens community.
No one should enter into it lightly or selfishly
but reverently and responsibly in the sight of almighty God.

N and N are now to enter this way of life.
They will each give their consent to the other
and make solemn vows,
and in token of this they will [each] give and receive a ring.
We pray with them that the Holy Spirit will guide
    and strengthen them,
that they may fulfil God's purposes
for the whole of their earthly life together.

The Declarations

First, I am required to ask anyone present who knows a reason
why these persons may not lawfully marry, to declare it now.

The minister says to the couple

The vows you are about to take are to be made in the presence
    of God,
who is judge of all and knows all the secrets of our hearts;
therefore if either of you knows a reason why you may not
    lawfully marry,
you must declare it now.

The minister says to the bridegroom

N, will you take N to be your wife?
Will you love her, comfort her, honour and protect her,
and, forsaking all others,
be faithful to her as long as you both shall live?

He answers

I will.

The minister says to the bride

N, will you take N to be your husband?
Will you love him, comfort him, honour and protect him,
and, forsaking all others,
be faithful to him as long as you both shall live?

She answers

I will.

The minister says to the congregation

Will you, the families and friends of N and N,
support and uphold them in their marriage
now and in the years to come?

All   **We will.**

The Collect

*The minister invites the people to pray, silence is kept
and the minister says the Collect*

God our Father,
from the beginning
you have blessed creation with abundant life.
Pour out your blessings upon *N* and *N,*
that they may be joined in mutual love and companionship,
in holiness and commitment to each other.
We ask this through our Lord Jesus Christ your Son,
who is alive and reigns with you,
in the unity of the Holy Spirit,
one God, now and for ever.

All **Amen.**

Readings

*At least one reading from the Bible is used.
A selection of readings is found on pages 16–28.*

Sermon

¶ The Marriage

A hymn may be sung.

The couple stand before the minister.

The Vows

The minister introduces the vows in these or similar words

N and N, I now invite you to join hands and make your vows,
in the presence of God and his people.

The bride and bridegroom face each other.
The bridegroom takes the bride's right hand in his.

These words, or those on pages 29–30, are used

I, N, take you, N,
to be my wife,
to have and to hold
from this day forward;
for better, for worse,
for richer, for poorer,
in sickness and in health,
to love and to cherish,
till death us do part;
according to God's holy law.
In the presence of God I make this vow.

They loose hands.
The bride takes the bridegroom's right hand in hers, and says

I, N, take you, N,
to be my husband,
to have and to hold
from this day forward;
for better, for worse,
for richer, for poorer,
in sickness and in health,
to love and to cherish,
till death us do part;
according to God's holy law.
In the presence of God I make this vow.

They loose hands.

The Giving of Rings

The minister receives the ring(s), and says this prayer or the prayer on page 30

Heavenly Father, by your blessing
let *these rings* be to N and N
a symbol of unending love and faithfulness,
to remind them of the vow and covenant
which they have made this day
through Jesus Christ our Lord.

All **Amen.**

The bridegroom places the ring on the fourth finger of the bride's left hand and, holding it there, says

N, I give you this ring
as a sign of our marriage.
With my body I honour you,
all that I am I give to you,
and all that I have I share with you,
within the love of God,
Father, Son and Holy Spirit.

If rings are exchanged, they loose hands and the bride places a ring on the fourth finger of the bridegroom's left hand and, holding it there, says

N, I give you this ring
as a sign of our marriage.
With my body I honour you,
all that I am I give to you,
and all that I have I share with you,
within the love of God,
Father, Son and Holy Spirit.

If only one ring is used, before they loose hands the bride says

N, I receive this ring
as a sign of our marriage.
With my body I honour you,
all that I am I give to you,
and all that I have I share with you,
within the love of God,
Father, Son and Holy Spirit.

The Proclamation

The minister addresses the people

In the presence of God, and before this congregation,
N and *N* have given their consent
and made their marriage vows to each other.
They have declared their marriage by the joining of hands
and by the giving and receiving of *rings*.
I therefore proclaim that they are husband and wife.

The minister joins their right hands together and says

Those whom God has joined together let no one put asunder.

The Blessing of the Marriage

The husband and wife kneel. The minister may use the following blessing or one of those on pages 31–32 in this booklet or pages 152–155 in Common Worship: Pastoral Services.

Blessed are you, O Lord our God,
for you have created joy and gladness,
pleasure and delight, love, peace and fellowship.
Pour out the abundance of your blessing
upon N and N in their new life together.
Let their love for each other be a seal upon their hearts
and a crown upon their heads.
Bless them in their work and in their companionship;
awake and asleep,
in joy and in sorrow,
in life and in death.
Finally, in your mercy, bring them to that banquet
where your saints feast for ever in your heavenly home.
We ask this through Jesus Christ your Son, our Lord,
who lives and reigns with you and the Holy Spirit,
one God, now and for ever.

All **Amen.**

The minister says to the couple

God the Father,
God the Son,
God the Holy Spirit,
bless, preserve and keep you;
the Lord mercifully grant you the riches of his grace,
that you may please him both in body and soul,
and, living together in faith and love,
may receive the blessings of eternal life.

All **Amen.**

Registration of the Marriage

See Note 10 on page 40.

A hymn or psalm may be used (see pages 27–28).

Prayers

These or other suitable prayers are used (see Note 9 on page 39 in this booklet and pages 156–168 in Common Worship: Pastoral Services*). The prayers usually include these concerns and may follow this sequence:*

¶   *Thanksgiving*

¶   *Spiritual growth*

¶   *Faithfulness, joy, love, forgiveness and healing*

¶   *Children, other family members and friends*

Faithful God,
holy and eternal,
source of life and spring of love,
we thank and praise you for bringing *N* and *N* to this day,
and we pray for them.
Lord of life and love:

All   **hear our prayer.**

May their marriage be life-giving and life-long,
enriched by your presence and strengthened by your grace;
may they bring comfort and confidence to each other
in faithfulness and trust.
Lord of life and love:

All   **hear our prayer.**

May the hospitality of their home
bring refreshment and joy to all around them;
may their love overflow to neighbours in need
and embrace those in distress.
Lord of life and love:

All   **hear our prayer.**

May they discern in your word
order and purpose for their lives;
and may the power of your Holy Spirit
lead them in truth and defend them in adversity.
Lord of life and love:

All   **hear our prayer.**

May they nurture their family with devotion,
see their children grow in body, mind and spirit
and come at last to the end of their lives
with hearts content and in joyful anticipation of heaven.
Lord of life and love:

All **hear our prayer.**

The prayers conclude with the Lord's Prayer.

As our Saviour taught us, so we pray

All **Our Father in heaven,**
hallowed be your name,
your kingdom come,
your will be done,
on earth as in heaven.
Give us today our daily bread.
Forgive us our sins
as we forgive those who sin against us.
Lead us not into temptation
but deliver us from evil.
For the kingdom, the power,
and the glory are yours
now and for ever.
Amen.

(or)

Let us pray with confidence as our Saviour has taught us

All **Our Father, who art in heaven,**
hallowed be thy name;
thy kingdom come;
thy will be done;
on earth as it is in heaven.
Give us this day our daily bread.
And forgive us our trespasses,
as we forgive those who trespass against us.
And lead us not into temptation;
but deliver us from evil.
For thine is the kingdom,
the power and the glory,
for ever and ever.
Amen.

A hymn may be sung.

The Dismissal

God the Holy Trinity make *you* strong in faith and love,
defend *you* on every side, and guide *you* in truth and peace;
and the blessing of God almighty,
the Father, the Son, and the Holy Spirit,
be among *you* and remain with *you* always.

All **Amen.**

The Marriage Service within a Celebration of Holy Communion

Structure

¶ **The Gathering**
The Welcome
Prayers of Penitence
Preface
The Declarations
The Collect

¶ **The Liturgy of the Word**
Readings
Gospel Reading
Sermon

¶ **The Marriage**
The Vows
The Giving of Rings
The Proclamation
† The Blessing of the Marriage
Registration of the Marriage
Prayers

¶ **The Liturgy of the Sacrament**
The Peace
Preparation of the Table
Taking of the Bread and Wine
The Eucharistic Prayer
The Lord's Prayer
　　† The Blessing of the Marriage
Breaking of the Bread
Giving of Communion
Prayer after Communion

¶ **The Dismissal**

† indicates alternative position allowed and shown indented in italics

For a full text of the Marriage Service within a Celebration of Holy Communion, see pages 116–131 in Common Worship: Pastoral Services.

¶ Confession and Absolution

When a marriage takes place within a Celebration of Holy Communion,
one of the following forms of Confession and Absolution may be used.

Either

All   **Lord our God,**
in our sin we have avoided your call.
Our love for you is like a morning cloud,
like the dew that goes away early.
Have mercy on us;
deliver us from judgement;
bind up our wounds
and revive us;
in Jesus Christ our Lord.
Amen.

The president says

The Lord forgive *you your* sin,
unite *you* in the love which took Christ to the cross,
and bring *you* in the Spirit to his wedding feast in heaven.

All   **Amen.**

(or)

Lord, in our weakness you are our strength.
Lord, have mercy.

All   **Lord, have mercy.**

Lord, when we stumble, you raise us up.
Christ, have mercy.

All   **Christ, have mercy.**

Lord, when we fail, you give us new life.
Lord, have mercy.

All   **Lord, have mercy.**

The president says

May God in his goodness forgive *us our* sins,
grant *us* strength in *our* weakness,
and bring *us* to eternal life,
through Jesus Christ our Lord.

All   **Amen.**

Supplementary Texts

¶ *Alternative Preface*

We have come together in the presence of God, to witness the marriage of N and N, to ask his blessing on them, and to share in their joy. Our Lord Jesus Christ was himself a guest at a wedding in Cana of Galilee, and through his Spirit he is with us now.

The Bible teaches us that marriage is a gift of God in creation and a means of his grace, a holy mystery in which man and woman become one flesh. It is God's purpose that, as husband and wife give themselves to each other in love throughout their lives, they shall be united in that love as Christ is united with his Church.

Marriage is given, that husband and wife may comfort and help each other, living faithfully together in need and in plenty, in sorrow and in joy. It is given, that with delight and tenderness they may know each other in love, and, through the joy of their bodily union, may strengthen the union of their hearts and lives. It is given as the foundation of family life in which children may be born and nurtured in accordance with God's will, to his praise and glory.

In marriage husband and wife belong to one another, and they begin a new life together in the community. It is a way of life that all should honour; and it must not be undertaken carelessly, lightly, or selfishly, but reverently, responsibly, and after serious thought.

This is the way of life, created and hallowed by God, that N and N are now to begin. They will each give their consent to the other; they will join hands and exchange solemn vows, and in token of this they will [each] give and receive a ring.

Therefore, on this their wedding day we pray with them, that, strengthened and guided by God, they may fulfil his purpose for the whole of their earthly life together.

¶ *Readings and Psalms*

Any suitable translation may be used.

Old Testament and Apocrypha

Genesis 1.26-28

Then God said, 'Let us make humankind in our image, according to our likeness; and let them have dominion over the fish of the sea, and over the birds of the air, and over the cattle, and over all the wild animals of the earth, and over every creeping thing that creeps upon the earth.'

So God created humankind in his image,
in the image of God he created them;
male and female he created them.

God blessed them, and God said to them, 'Be fruitful and multiply, and fill the earth and subdue it; and have dominion over the fish of the sea and over the birds of the air and over every living thing that moves upon the earth.'

Song of Solomon 2.10-13; 8.6,7

My beloved speaks and says to me:
'Arise, my love, my fair one,
and come away;
for now the winter is past,
the rain is over and gone.
The flowers appear on the earth;
the time of singing has come,
and the voice of the turtle dove
is heard in our land.
The fig tree puts forth its figs,
and the vines are in blossom;
they give forth fragrance.
Arise, my love, my fair one,
and come away.'

Set me as a seal upon your heart,
as a seal upon your arm;
for love is strong as death,
passion fierce as the grave.
Its flashes are flashes of fire,
a raging flame.
Many waters cannot quench love,
neither can floods drown it.
If one offered for love
all the wealth of one's house,
it would be utterly scorned.

Jeremiah 31.31-34

The days are surely coming, says the Lord, when I will make a
new covenant with the house of Israel and the house of Judah.
It will not be like the covenant that I made with their ancestors
when I took them by the hand to bring them out of the land of
Egypt – a covenant that they broke, though I was their husband,
says the Lord. But this is the covenant that I will make with the
house of Israel after those days, says the Lord: I will put my law
within them, and I will write it on their hearts; and I will be their
God, and they shall be my people. No longer shall they teach one
another, or say to each other, 'Know the Lord', for they shall all
know me, from the least of them to the greatest, says the Lord;
for I will forgive their iniquity, and remember their sin no more.

Tobit 8.4-8

When the parents had gone out and shut the door of the room,
Tobias got out of bed and said to Sarah, 'Sister, get up, and let us
pray and implore our Lord that he grant us mercy and safety.'
So she got up, and they began to pray and implore that they might
be kept safe. Tobias began by saying,
'Blessed are you, O God of our ancestors,
and blessed is your name in all generations for ever.
Let the heavens and the whole creation bless you for ever.
You made Adam, and for him you made his wife Eve
as a helper and support.
From the two of them the human race has sprung.
You said, "It is not good that the man should be alone;
let us make a helper for him like himself."

I now am taking this kinswoman of mine,
not because of lust,
but with sincerity.
Grant that she and I may find mercy
and that we may grow old together.'

And they both said, 'Amen, amen.'

Epistle

Romans 7.1,2,9-18

Do you not know, brothers and sisters – for I am speaking to those who know the law – that the law is binding on a person only during that person's lifetime? Thus a married woman is bound by the law to her husband as long as he lives; but if her husband dies, she is discharged from the law concerning the husband.

I was once alive apart from the law, but when the commandment came, sin revived and I died, and the very commandment that promised life proved to be death to me. For sin, seizing an opportunity in the commandment, deceived me and through it killed me. So the law is holy, and the commandment is holy and just and good.

Did what is good, then, bring death to me? By no means! It was sin, working death in me through what is good, in order that sin might be shown to be sin, and through the commandment might become sinful beyond measure.

For we know that the law is spiritual; but I am of the flesh, sold into slavery under sin. I do not understand my own actions. For I do not do what I want, but I do the very thing I hate. Now if I do what I do not want, I agree that the law is good. But in fact it is no longer I that do it, but sin that dwells within me. For I know that nothing good dwells within me, that is, in my flesh. I can will what is right, but I cannot do it.

Romans 8.31-35,37-39

What then are we to say about these things? If God is for us, who is against us? He who did not withhold his own Son, but gave him up for all of us, will he not with him also give us everything else? Who will bring any charge against God's elect? It is God who justifies. Who is to condemn? It is Christ Jesus, who died, yes, who was raised, who is at the right hand of God, who indeed intercedes for us. Who will separate us from the love of Christ? Will hardship, or distress, or persecution, or famine, or nakedness, or peril, or sword?

No, in all these things we are more than conquerors through him who loved us. For I am convinced that neither death, nor life, nor angels, nor rulers, nor things present, nor things to come, nor powers, nor height, nor depth, nor anything else in all creation, will be able to separate us from the love of God in Christ Jesus our Lord.

Romans 12.1,2,9-13

I appeal to you therefore, brothers and sisters, by the mercies of God, to present your bodies as a living sacrifice, holy and acceptable to God, which is your spiritual worship. Do not be conformed to this world, but be transformed by the renewing of your minds, so that you may discern what is the will of God – what is good and acceptable and perfect.

Let love be genuine; hate what is evil, hold fast to what is good; love one another with mutual affection; outdo one another in showing honour. Do not lag in zeal, be ardent in spirit, serve the Lord. Rejoice in hope, be patient in suffering, persevere in prayer. Contribute to the needs of the saints; extend hospitality to strangers.

Romans 15.1-3,5-7,13

We who are strong ought to put up with the failings of the weak, and not to please ourselves. Each of us must please our neighbour for the good purpose of building up the neighbour. For Christ did not please himself; but, as it is written, 'The insults of those who insult you have fallen on me.'

May the God of steadfastness and encouragement grant you to live in harmony with one another, in accordance with Christ Jesus, so that together you may with one voice glorify the God and Father of our Lord Jesus Christ. Welcome one another, therefore, just as Christ has welcomed you, for the glory of God.

May the God of hope fill you with all joy and peace in believing, so that you may abound in hope by the power of the Holy Spirit.

1 Corinthians 13

If I speak in the tongues of mortals and of angels, but do not have love, I am a noisy gong or a clanging cymbal. And if I have prophetic powers, and understand all mysteries and all knowledge, and if I have all faith, so as to remove mountains, but do not have love, I am nothing. If I give away all my possessions, and if I hand over my body so that I may boast, but do not have love, I gain nothing.

Love is patient; love is kind; love is not envious or boastful or arrogant or rude. It does not insist on its own way; it is not irritable or resentful; it does not rejoice in wrongdoing, but rejoices in the truth. It bears all things, believes all things, hopes all things, endures all things.

Love never ends. But as for prophecies, they will come to an end; as for tongues, they will cease; as for knowledge, it will come to an end. For we know only in part, and we prophesy only in part; but when the complete comes, the partial will come to an end. When I was a child, I spoke like a child, I thought like a child, I reasoned like a child; when I became an adult, I put an end to childish ways. For now we see in a mirror, dimly, but then we will see face to face. Now I know only in part; then I will know fully, even as I have been fully known. And now faith, hope, and love abide, these three; and the greatest of these is love.

Ephesians 3.14-end

I bow my knees before the Father, from whom every family in heaven and on earth takes its name. I pray that, according to the riches of his glory, he may grant that you may be strengthened in your inner being with power through his Spirit, and that Christ may dwell in your hearts through faith, as you are being rooted and grounded in love. I pray that you may have the power to comprehend, with all the saints, what is the breadth and length and height and depth, and to know the love of Christ that surpasses knowledge, so that you may be filled with all the fullness of God.

Now to him who by the power at work within us is able to accomplish abundantly far more than all we can ask or imagine, to him be glory in the church and in Christ Jesus to all generations, for ever and ever. Amen.

Ephesians 4.1-6

I, the prisoner in the Lord, beg you to lead a life worthy of the calling to which you have been called, with all humility and gentleness, with patience, bearing with one another in love, making every effort to maintain the unity of the Spirit in the bond of peace. There is one body and one Spirit, just as you were called to the one hope of your calling, one Lord, one faith, one baptism, one God and Father of all, who is above all and through all and in all.

Ephesians 5.21-end

Be subject to one another out of reverence for Christ.

Wives, be subject to your husbands as you are to the Lord. For the husband is the head of the wife just as Christ is the head of the church, the body of which he is the Saviour. Just as the church is subject to Christ, so also wives ought to be, in everything, to their husbands.

Husbands, love your wives, just as Christ loved the church and gave himself up for her, in order to make her holy by cleansing her with the washing of water by the word, so as to present the church to himself in splendour, without a spot or wrinkle or anything of the kind – yes, so that she may be holy and without blemish. In the same way, husbands should love their wives as they do their own bodies. He who loves his wife loves himself. For no one ever hates his own body, but he nourishes and tenderly cares for it, just as Christ does for the church, because we are members of his body. 'For this reason a man will leave his father and mother and be joined to his wife, and the two will become one flesh.' This is a great mystery, and I am applying it to Christ and the church. Each of you, however, should love his wife as himself, and a wife should respect her husband.

Philippians 4.4-9

Rejoice in the Lord always; again I will say, Rejoice. Let your gentleness be known to everyone. The Lord is near. Do not worry about anything, but in everything by prayer and supplication with thanksgiving let your requests be made known to God. And the peace of God, which surpasses all understanding, will guard your hearts and your minds in Christ Jesus.

Finally, beloved, whatever is true, whatever is honourable, whatever is just, whatever is pure, whatever is pleasing, whatever is commendable, if there is any excellence and if there is anything worthy of praise, think about these things. Keep on doing the things that you have learned and received and heard and seen in me, and the God of peace will be with you.

Colossians 3.12-17

As God's chosen ones, holy and beloved, clothe yourselves with compassion, kindness, humility, meekness, and patience. Bear with one another and, if anyone has a complaint against another, forgive each other; just as the Lord has forgiven you, so you also must forgive. Above all, clothe yourselves with love, which binds everything together in perfect harmony. And let the peace of Christ rule in your hearts, to which indeed you were called in the one body. And be thankful. Let the word of Christ dwell in you richly; teach and admonish one another in all wisdom; and with gratitude in your hearts sing psalms, hymns, and spiritual songs to God. And whatever you do, in word or deed, do everything in the name of the Lord Jesus, giving thanks to God the Father through him.

I John 3.18-end

Little children, let us love, not in word or speech, but in truth and action. And by this we will know that we are from the truth and will reassure our hearts before him whenever our hearts condemn us; for God is greater than our hearts, and he knows everything. Beloved, if our hearts do not condemn us, we have boldness before God; and we receive from him whatever we ask, because we obey his commandments and do what pleases him.

And this is his commandment, that we should believe in the name of his Son Jesus Christ and love one another, just as he has commanded us. All who obey his commandments abide in him, and he abides in them. And by this we know that he abides in us, by the Spirit that he has given us.

I John 4.7-12

Beloved, let us love one another, because love is from God; everyone who loves is born of God and knows God. Whoever does not love does not know God, for God is love. God's love was revealed among us in this way: God sent his only Son into the world so that we might live through him. In this is love, not that we loved God but that he loved us and sent his Son to be the atoning sacrifice for our sins. Beloved, since God loved us so much, we also ought to love one another. No one has ever seen God; if we love one another, God lives in us, and his love is perfected in us.

Gospel

Matthew 5.1-10

When Jesus saw the crowds, he went up the mountain; and after he sat down, his disciples came to him. Then he began to speak, and taught them, saying:

'Blessed are the poor in spirit, for theirs is the kingdom of heaven.
Blessed are those who mourn, for they will be comforted.
Blessed are the meek, for they will inherit the earth.
Blessed are those who hunger and thirst for righteousness,
    for they will be filled.
Blessed are the merciful, for they will receive mercy.
Blessed are the pure in heart, for they will see God.
Blessed are the peacemakers, for they will be called children of God.
Blessed are those who are persecuted for righteousness' sake,
    for theirs is the kingdom of heaven.'

Matthew 7.21,24-end

Jesus said, 'Not everyone who says to me, "Lord, Lord", will enter the kingdom of heaven, but only one who does the will of my Father in heaven.

'Everyone then who hears these words of mine and acts on them will be like a wise man who built his house on rock. The rain fell, the floods came, and the winds blew and beat on that house, but it did not fall, because it had been founded on rock. And everyone who hears these words of mine and does not act on them will be like a foolish man who built his house on sand. The rain fell, and the floods came, and the winds blew and beat against that house, and it fell – and great was its fall!'

Now when Jesus had finished saying these things, the crowds were astounded at his teaching, for he taught them as one having authority, and not as their scribes.

Mark 10.6-9, 13-16

Jesus said, 'From the beginning of creation, "God made them male and female." "For this reason a man shall leave his father and mother and be joined to his wife, and the two shall become one flesh." So they are no longer two, but one flesh. Therefore what God has joined together, let no one separate.'

People were bringing little children to him in order that he might touch them; and the disciples spoke sternly to them. But when Jesus saw this, he was indignant and said to them, 'Let the little children come to me; do not stop them; for it is to such as these that the kingdom of God belongs. Truly I tell you, whoever does not receive the kingdom of God as a little child will never enter it.' And he took them up in his arms, laid his hands on them, and blessed them.

John 2.1-11

On the third day there was a wedding in Cana of Galilee, and the mother of Jesus was there. Jesus and his disciples had also been invited to the wedding. When the wine gave out, the mother of Jesus said to him, 'They have no wine.' And Jesus said to her, 'Woman, what concern is that to you and to me? My hour has not yet come.' His mother said to the servants, 'Do whatever he tells you.' Now standing there were six stone water-jars for the Jewish rites of purification, each holding twenty or thirty gallons. Jesus said to them, 'Fill the jars with water.' And they filled them up to the brim. He said to them, 'Now draw some out, and take it to the chief steward.' So they took it. When the steward tasted the water that had become wine, and did not know where it came from (though the servants who had drawn the water knew), the steward called the bridegroom and said to him, 'Everyone serves the good wine first, and then the inferior wine after the guests have become drunk. But you have kept the good wine until now.' Jesus did this, the first of his signs, in Cana of Galilee, and revealed his glory; and his disciples believed in him.

John 15.1-8

Jesus said to his disciples: 'I am the true vine, and my Father is the vinegrower. He removes every branch in me that bears no fruit. Every branch that bears fruit he prunes to make it bear more fruit. You have already been cleansed by the word that I have spoken to you. Abide in me as I abide in you. Just as the branch cannot bear fruit by itself unless it abides in the vine, neither can you unless you abide in me. I am the vine, you are the branches. Those who abide in me and I in them bear much fruit, because apart from me you can do nothing. Whoever does not abide in me is thrown away like a branch and withers; such branches are gathered, thrown into the fire, and burned. If you abide in me, and my words abide in you, ask for whatever you wish, and it will be done for you. My Father is glorified by this, that you bear much fruit and become my disciples.'

John 15.9-17

Jesus said to his disciples: 'As the Father has loved me, so I have loved you; abide in my love. If you keep my commandments, you will abide in my love, just as I have kept my Father's commandments and abide in his love. I have said these things to you so that my joy may be in you, and that your joy may be complete.

This is my commandment, that you love one another as I have loved you. No one has greater love than this, to lay down one's life for one's friends. You are my friends if you do what I command you. I do not call you servants any longer, because the servant does not know what the master is doing; but I have called you friends, because I have made known to you everything that I have heard from my Father. You did not choose me but I chose you. And I appointed you to go and bear fruit, fruit that will last, so that the Father will give you whatever you ask him in my name. I am giving you these commands so that you may love one another.'

Psalms

Psalm 67

1   God be gracious to us and bless us ♦
     and make his face to shine upon us,

2   That your way may be known upon earth, ♦
     your saving power among all nations.

3   *Let the peoples praise you, O God;* ♦
     let all the peoples praise you.

4   O let the nations rejoice and be glad, ♦
     for you will judge the peoples righteously
        and govern the nations upon earth.

5   *Let the peoples praise you, O God;* ♦
     let all the peoples praise you.

6   Then shall the earth bring forth her increase, ♦
     and God, our own God, will bless us.

7   God will bless us, ♦
     and all the ends of the earth shall fear him.

Psalm 121

1   I lift up my eyes to the hills; ♦
     from where is my help to come?

2   My help comes from the Lord, ♦
     the maker of heaven and earth.

3   He will not suffer your foot to stumble; ♦
     he who watches over you will not sleep.

4   Behold, he who keeps watch over Israel ♦
     shall neither slumber nor sleep.

5   The Lord himself watches over you; ♦
     the Lord is your shade at your right hand,

6   So that the sun shall not strike you by day, ♦
     neither the moon by night.

7   The Lord shall keep you from all evil; ♦
     it is he who shall keep your soul.

8   The Lord shall keep watch over your going out
        and your coming in, ♦
     from this time forth for evermore.

1 Unless the Lord builds the house, ♦
   those who build it labour in vain.

2 Unless the Lord keeps the city, ♦
   the guard keeps watch in vain.

3 It is in vain that you hasten to rise up early
         and go so late to rest, eating the bread of toil, ♦
   for he gives his beloved sleep.

4 Children are a heritage from the Lord ♦
   and the fruit of the womb is his gift.

5 Like arrows in the hand of a warrior, ♦
   so are the children of one's youth.

6 Happy are those who have their quiver full of them: ♦
   they shall not be put to shame
         when they dispute with their enemies in the gate.

Psalm 128

1 Blessed are all those who fear the Lord, ♦
   and walk in his ways.

2 You shall eat the fruit of the toil of your hands; ♦
   it shall go well with you, and happy shall you be.

3 Your wife within your house
         shall be like a fruitful vine; ♦
   your children round your table,
         like fresh olive branches.

4 Thus shall the one be blest ♦
   who fears the Lord.

5 The Lord from out of Zion bless you, ♦
   that you may see Jerusalem in prosperity
         all the days of your life.

6 May you see your children's children, ♦
   and may there be peace upon Israel.

¶ *Alternative Vows*

The bridegroom takes the bride's right hand in his, and says

I, *N*, take you, *N*,
to be my wife,
to have and to hold
from this day forward;
for better, for worse,
for richer, for poorer,
in sickness and in health,
to love and to cherish,
till death us do part,
according to God's holy law.
In the presence of God I make this vow.

They loose hands.
The bride takes the bridegroom's right hand in hers, and says

I, *N*, take you, *N*,
to be my husband,
to have and to hold
from this day forward;
for better, for worse,
for richer, for poorer,
in sickness and in health,
to love, cherish, and obey,
till death us do part,
according to God's holy law.
In the presence of God I make this vow.

The bridegroom takes the bride's right hand in his, and says

I, *N*, take thee, *N*, to my wedded wife, to have and to hold from this day forward, for better for worse, for richer for poorer, in sickness and in health, to love and to cherish, till death us do part, according to God's holy ordinance; and thereto I plight thee my troth.

They loose hands.
The bride takes the bridegroom's right hand in hers, and says

I, *N*, take thee, *N*, to my wedded husband, to have and to hold from this day forward, for better for worse, for richer for poorer, in sickness and in health, to love, cherish, and to obey, till death us do part, according to God's holy ordinance; and thereto I give thee my troth.

[*If desired, the word 'obey' may be omitted, as follows*

I, *N*, take thee, *N*, to my wedded husband, to have and to hold from this day forward, for better for worse, for richer for poorer, in sickness and in health, to love and to cherish, till death us do part, according to God's holy ordinance; and thereto I give thee my troth.]

¶ *Prayer at the Giving of the Ring(s)*

Heavenly Father, source of everlasting love,
revealed to us in Jesus Christ
    and poured into our hearts through your Holy Spirit;
that love which many waters cannot quench,
    neither the floods drown;
that love which is patient and kind, enduring all things without end;
by your blessing, let these rings be to *N* and *N*
symbols to remind them of the covenant made this day
through your grace in the love of your Son
and in the power of your Spirit.

All **Amen.**

¶ The Blessing of the Marriage

The following form or one of those on pages 152–153 in Common Worship: Pastoral Services *may be used (see also page 32)*

Blessed are you, Lord our God,
God of love, creator of all.

All **Blessed be God for ever.**

Bridegroom Blessed are you, Lord our God,
you make us in your image and likeness.

All **Blessed be God for ever.**

Bride Blessed are you, Lord our God,
you make man and woman to reflect your glory.

All **Blessed be God for ever.**

Bridegroom Blessed are you, Lord our God,
you make us for joy and promise us life.

All **Blessed be God for ever.**

Bride Blessed are you, Lord our God,
you create a people to know your love.

All **Blessed be God for ever.**

Minister May N and N enjoy the blessing of your kingdom.
Give them faith and joy in their marriage.
Blessed are you, Lord our God,
you give joy to bride and groom.

All **Blessed be God for ever.**

May their love be fruitful
and their home a place of peace.
Blessed are you, Lord our God,
you make marriage a sign of your love.

All **Blessed be God for ever.**

May they know the love of the Father,
the life of the Son,
and the joy of the Spirit.
Blessed are you, Lord our God,
Lover, Beloved and Friend of Love.

All **Blessed be God for ever.**

The following form may be added to any of the blessings,
or may be used on its own

Blessed are you, heavenly Father.

All **You give joy to bridegroom and bride.**

Blessed are you, Lord Jesus Christ.

All **You bring life to the world.**

Blessed are you, Holy Spirit of God.

All **You bind us together in love.**

Blessed are you, Father, Son, and Holy Spirit, now and for ever.

All **Amen.**

¶ Prayers

The prayers usually include these concerns and may follow
this sequence:

¶ *Thanksgiving*

¶ *Spiritual growth*

¶ *Faithfulness, joy, love, forgiveness and healing*

¶ *Children, other family members and friends*

Suitable prayers are suggested on pages 156–168 in Common
Worship: Pastoral Services *(see also Note 9 on page 39 in this booklet).*

These responses may be used

Lord, hear us.
All **Lord, graciously hear us.**

(or)

Lord, in your mercy
All **hear our prayer.**

And at the end

Almighty God, you have promised to hear our prayers.
All **Grant that what we have asked in faith**
we may by your grace receive,
through Jesus Christ our Lord. Amen.

A Song of Solomon

Refrain:

All **Many waters cannot quench love;**
neither can the floods drown it.

1   Set me as a seal upon your heart, ♦
    as a seal upon your arm;

2   For love is strong as death, passion fierce as the grave; ♦
    its flashes are flashes of fire, a raging flame.

3   Many waters cannot quench love, ♦
    neither can the floods drown it.

4   If all the wealth of our house were offered for love, ♦
    it would be utterly scorned.   *cf Song of Solomon 8.6-7*

   Glory to the Father and to the Son
   and to the Holy Spirit;
   as it was in the beginning is now
   and shall be for ever. Amen.

A Song of the Bride

Refrain:

All **God makes righteousness and praise
blossom before all the nations.**

1   I will greatly rejoice in the Lord, ♦
      my soul shall exult in my God;

2   Who has clothed me with the garments of salvation, ♦
      and has covered me with the cloak of integrity,

3   As a bridegroom decks himself with a garland, ♦
      and as a bride adorns herself with her jewels.

4   For as the earth puts forth her blossom, ♦
      and as seeds in the garden spring up,

5   So shall God make righteousness and praise ♦
      blossom before all the nations.

6   For Zion's sake I will not keep silent, ♦
      and for Jerusalem's sake I will not rest,

7   Until her deliverance shines out like the dawn, ♦
      and her salvation as a burning torch.

8   The nations shall see your deliverance, ♦
      and all rulers shall see your glory;

9   Then you shall be called by a new name ♦
      which the mouth of God will give.

10   You shall be a crown of glory in the hand of the Lord, ♦
      a royal diadem in the hand of your God.   *Isaiah 61.10,11; 62.1-3*

      Glory to the Father and to the Son
      and to the Holy Spirit;
      as it was in the beginning is now
      and shall be for ever.   Amen.

Magnificat (The Song of Mary)

1   My soul proclaims the greatness of the Lord,
      my spirit rejoices in God my Saviour; ✦
   he has looked with favour on his lowly servant.

2   From this day all generations will call me blessed; ✦
   the Almighty has done great things for me
      and holy is his name.

3   He has mercy on those who fear him, ✦
   from generation to generation.

4   He has shown strength with his arm ✦
   and has scattered the proud in their conceit,

5   Casting down the mighty from their thrones ✦
   and lifting up the lowly.

6   He has filled the hungry with good things ✦
   and sent the rich away empty.

7   He has come to the aid of his servant Israel, ✦
   to remember his promise of mercy,

8   The promise made to our ancestors, ✦
   to Abraham and his children for ever.   *Luke 1.46-55*

Glory to the Father and to the Son
and to the Holy Spirit;
as it was in the beginning is now
and shall be for ever. Amen.

A Song of the Lamb

Refrain:

All **Let us rejoice and exult**
and give glory and homage to our God.

1   Salvation and glory and power belong to our God, ♦
    whose judgements are true and just.

2   Praise our God, all you his servants, ♦
    all who fear him, both small and great.

3   The Lord our God, the Almighty, reigns: ♦
    let us rejoice and exult and give him the glory.

4   For the marriage of the Lamb has come ♦
    and his bride has made herself ready.

5   Blessed are those who are invited ♦
    to the wedding banquet of the Lamb.   *Revelation 19.1b,2b,5b,6b,7,9b*

    To the One who sits on the throne and to the Lamb ♦
    be blessing and honour and glory and might,
        for ever and ever. Amen.

Notes to the Marriage Service

1   **Preparation**
    It is the custom and practice of the Church of England to offer
    preparation for marriage for couples who are soon to be married,
    as well as to be available for support and counselling in the years
    that follow.

2   **The Banns**
    The banns are to be published in the church on three Sundays at
    the time of Divine Service by the officiant in the form set out in
    The Book of Common Prayer or in the following form:

    > I publish the banns of marriage between *NN* of … and *NN* of …
    > This is the *first / second / third* time of asking. If any of you know
    > any reason in law why they may not marry each other you are
    > to declare it.
    > We pray for these couples *(or N and N)* as they prepare for
    > their wedding*(s)*.

    A suitable prayer may be said (see page 135 in *Common Worship:
    Pastoral Services*).

3   **Hymns and Canticles**
    These may be used at suitable points during the service.

4   **Entry**
    The bride may enter the church escorted by her father or
    a representative of the family, or the bride and groom may
    enter church together.

5   **Readings and Sermon**
    At least one reading from the Bible must be used. Suggested
    readings are printed on pages 16–28. If occasion demands,
    either the Sermon or the Readings and Sermon may come
    after the Blessing of the Marriage. Chairs may be provided
    for the bride and bridegroom.

6   **'Giving Away'**
    This traditional ceremony is optional. Immediately before
    the couple exchange vows (page 6), the minister may ask:

    Who brings this woman to be married to this man?

    The bride's father (or mother, or another member of her family
    or a friend representing the family) gives the bride's right hand to
    the minister who puts it in the bridegroom's right hand.
    Alternatively, after the bride and bridegroom have made their
    Declarations, the minister may ask the parents of bride and
    bridegroom in these or similar words:

    N and N have declared their intention towards each other.
    As their parents,
    will you now entrust your son and daughter to one another
    as they come to be married?

    Both sets of parents respond:

    We will.

7   **The Declarations and the Vows**
    The *Book of Common Prayer* version of the Declarations, and/or the
    alternative vows on pages 29–30, may be used. The couple repeat
    the vows after the minister, or may read them. If preferred, the
    question to the bride, and her vow, may come before the question
    to the bridegroom and his vow.

8   **The Giving of Rings**
    If desired, the bride and bridegroom may each place a ring on the
    fourth finger of the other's hand, and may then say together the
    words '*N*, I give you this ring …'. The prayer on page 30 may be
    used instead of the prayer on page 7.

9   **The Prayers**
    Several forms of intercession are provided. Other suitable forms
    may be used, especially prayers which the couple have written or
    selected in co-operation with the minister. Whatever form is used,
    silence may be kept as part of the intercession. Free prayer may be
    offered.

10 **Registration of the Marriage**
The law requires that the Registers are filled in immediately after the solemnization of a marriage. This may take place either after the Blessing of the Marriage or at the end of the service.

11 **Holy Communion**
For communicant members of the Church it is appropriate that they receive communion soon after their marriage. For some this may make it appropriate for the marriage to take place within the context of a Celebration of Holy Communion.

12 **The Marriage Service within a Celebration of Holy Communion**
The Notes to the Order for the Celebration of Holy Communion, as well as the Notes to the Marriage Service, apply equally to this service. Texts are suggested at different points, but other suitable texts may be used. Authorized Prayers of Penitence may be used. In the Liturgy of the Word, there should be a Gospel reading, preceded by either one or two other readings from the Bible. If desired, the Blessing of the Marriage may take place between the Lord's Prayer and the Breaking of the Bread.

13 **Ecumenical Provisions**
Where a minister of another Christian Church is invited to assist at the Solemnization of Matrimony, the permissions and procedures set out in Canon B 43 are to be followed. The Church of England minister who solemnizes the marriage must establish the absence of impediment, direct the exchange of vows, declare the existence of the marriage, say the final blessing, and sign the registers. A minister invited to assist may say all or part of the opening address, lead the declarations of intent, supervise the exchange of rings, and join in the blessing of the marriage. He or she may also read a lesson and lead all or part of the prayers. Where the couple come from different Christian communions the bishop may authorize such variations to the marriage service as are set out in *An Order for the Marriage of Christians from Different Churches*, which is published separately.

General Rules for Regulating Authorized Forms of Service

1. Any reference in authorized provision to the use of hymns shall be construed as including the use of texts described as songs, chants, canticles.

2. If occasion requires, hymns may be sung at points other than those indicated in particular forms of service. Silence may be kept at points other than those indicated in particular forms of service.

3. Where rubrics indicate that a text is to be 'said' this must be understood to include 'or sung' and vice versa.

4. Where parts of a service make use of well-known and traditional texts, other translations or versions, particularly when used in musical compositions, may be used.

5. Local custom may be established and followed in respect of posture but regard should be had to indications in Notes attached to authorized forms of service that a particular posture is appropriate for some parts of that form of service.

6. On any occasion when the text of an alternative service authorized under the provisions of Canon B 2 provides for the Lord's Prayer to be said or sung, it may be used in the form included in *The Book of Common Prayer* or in either of the two other forms included in services in *Common Worship*. The further text included in Prayers for Various Occasions (page 106 in *Common Worship: Services and Prayers for the Church of England*) may be used on suitable occasions.

7. Normally on any occasion only one Collect is used.

8. At Baptisms, Confirmations, Ordinations and Marriages which take place on Principal Feasts, other Principal Holy Days and on Sundays of Advent, Lent and Easter, within the Celebration of the Holy Communion, the Readings of the day are used and the Collect of the Day is said, unless the bishop directs otherwise.

9. The Collects and Lectionary in *Common Worship* may, optionally, be used in conjunction with the days included in the Calendar of *The Book of Common Prayer*, notwithstanding any difference in the title or name of a Sunday, Holy Day or other observance included in both Calendars.

Authorization

¶   The following services and other material are authorized pursuant
to Canon B 2 of the Canons of the Church of England for use until
further resolution of the General Synod:

   ¶   The Marriage Service
   ¶   The Marriage Service within a Celebration of Holy Communion
   ¶   Supplementary Texts (Marriage)
   ¶   General Rules for Regulating Authorized Forms of Service

¶   The Canticles for the Marriage Service have been commended by
the House of Bishops of the General Synod pursuant to Canon B 2
of the Canons of the Church of England and are published with
the agreement of the House.

Under Canon B 4 it is open to each bishop to authorize, if he sees
fit, the form of service to be used within his diocese. He may specify
that the services shall be those commended by the House, or that
a diocesan form of them shall be used. If the bishop gives no
directions in this matter the priest remains free, subject to the
terms of Canon B 5, to make use of the services as commended
by the House.

Acknowledgements

The publisher gratefully acknowledges permission to reproduce copyright material in this book. Every effort has been made to trace and contact copyright holders. If there are any inadvertent omissions we apologize to those concerned and undertake to include suitable acknowledgements in all future editions.

Published sources include the following:

The Archbishops' Council of the Church of England: *The Prayer Book as Proposed in 1928* which is copyright © The Archbishops' Council of the Church of England.

Cambridge University Press: Extracts (and adapted extracts) from *The Book of Common Prayer*, the rights in which are vested in the Crown, are reproduced by permission of the Crown's Patentee, Cambridge University Press.

The Division of Christian Education of the National Council of Churches in the USA: Unless otherwise stated, Scripture quotations are from *The New Revised Standard Version of the Bible,* copyright © 1989 by the Division of Christian Education of the National Council of Churches in the USA. Used by permission. All rights reserved.

Thanks are also due to the following for permission to reproduce copyright material:

The Anglican Church in Aotearoa, New Zealand and Polynesia: Pastoral Introduction (p. iv). Adapted from *A New Zealand Prayer Book – He Karikia Mihinare O Aotearoa*, copyright © The Church of the Province of New Zealand 1989.

The Joint Liturgical Group of Great Britain: Blessing (p. 31) from *An Order of Marriage for Christians from Different Churches*, copyright © The Joint Liturgical Group of Great Britain, 1999. Used by permission.

Jubilate Hymns: Confession and Absolution (p. 14 top) from *Church Family Worship*. Words: Michael Perry © Mrs B Perry/ Jubilate Hymns 1986. Used by permission.